IN THE RED AND BROWN WATER

BY
TARELL ALV

★

DRAMATISTS
PLAY SERVICE
INC.

IN THE RED AND BROWN WATER
Copyright © 2013, Tarell Alvin McCraney

All Rights Reserved

SPECIAL NOTE

Anyone receiving permission to produce IN THE RED AND BROWN WATER is required to give credit to the Author as sole and exclusive Author of the Play on the title page of all programs distributed in connection with performances of the Play and in all instances in which the title of the Play appears, including printed or digital materials for advertising, publicizing or otherwise exploiting the Play and/or a production thereof. The name of the Author must appear on a separate line, in which no other name appears, immediately beneath the title and in size of type equal to 50% of the size of the largest, most prominent letter used for the title of the Play. No person, firm or entity may receive credit larger or more prominent than that accorded the Author. The following acknowledgments must appear on the title page of all programs distributed in connection with performances of the Play, and in all advertising and publicity in which full production credits appear:

IN THE RED AND BROWN WATER was originally produced by
Alliance Theatre, Atlanta, GA,
(Susan Booth, Artistic Director; Thomas Pechar, Managing Director).

U.K. stage premiere produced by the Young Vic Company.

World premiere of THE BROTHER/SISTER PLAYS produced by
the Public Theater
(Oskar Eustis, Artistic Director; Andrew D. Hamingson, Executive Director),
and McCarter Theatre Center
(Emily Mann, Artistic Director; Timothy J. Shields, Managing Director).

THE BROTHER/SISTER PLAYS were developed with the support of McCarter Theatre Center.

SPECIAL NOTE ON SONGS AND RECORDINGS

For performances of copyrighted songs, arrangements or recordings mentioned in these Plays, the permission of the copyright owner(s) must be obtained. Other songs, arrangements or recordings may be substituted provided permission from the copyright owner(s) of such songs, arrangements or recordings is obtained; or songs, arrangements or recordings in the public domain may be substituted.

2

2 my sisters

IN THE RED AND BROWN WATER was presented at the Public Theater (Oskar Eustis, Artistic Director; Andrew D. Hamingson, Executive Director) in association with McCarter Theatre Center (Emily Mann, Artistic Director; Timothy J. Shields, Managing Director) in New York City, opening on Novemeber 18, 2009. It was directed by Tina Landau; the set design was by James Schuette; the costume design was by Karen Perry; the lighting design was by Peter Kaczorowski; the sound design was by Lindsay Jones; and the vocal arrangements were by Zane Mark. The cast was as follows:

OYA .... Kianné Muschett
ELEGBA .... André Holland
OGUN .... Marc Damon Johnson
MAMA MOJA, THE WOMAN THAT
REMINDS YOU/NIA .... Heather Alicia Simms
AUNT ELEGUA .... Kimberly Hébert Gregory
SHUN .... Nikiya Mathis
SHANGO .... Sterling K. Brown
O LI ROON, THE MAN FROM STATE .... Sean Allan Krill
THE EGUNGUN .... Brian Tyree Henry

CHARACTERS

OYA begins the play a girl and ends it a woman,
a woman of color.

ELEGBA begins the play a boy and ends it a man,
godbrother to Oya, of Creole heritage.

OGUN, with Oya for a time, nephew of Aunt Elegua,
a man of color.

MAMA MOJA, THE WOMAN THAT REMINDS YOU,
mother of Oya, godmother to Elegba, a mother of color.

AUNT ELEGUA, Aunt to Ogun, godmother to Oya,
a woman of color.

NIA, girl from around the way.

SHUN, girl from around the way, friend to Nia,
a fair woman of color.

SHANGO, with Oya for a time, a dark man of color.

O LI ROON, THE MAN FROM STATE, a white man.

THE EGUNGUN, a DJ, a boy from around the way.

PLACE

Distant present.

TIME

San Pere, Louisiana.

NOTES

IN THE RED AND BROWN WATER draws on Yoruba traditions and stories both Caribbean and African.

If there is a space after a character name, it means there is a silent action or pause being played at that moment.

The stage directions in the characters' speech are meant to be said as well as played.

IN THE RED AND BROWN WATER

PROLOGUE

Lights come on.

The cast is standing in a line downstage.

The men all begin to hum, a sad sweet hum,

Thick like the early morning mist.

They move upstage.

Halfway through the journey

Oya is left center alone.

She lies down on the ground, holds her head

And stares up to the sky. Her lines are said from this position like a chant or moan.

The others continue upstage, speaking their lines, the men still humming.

Until finally they stand still.

The cast glows like a pantheon of deities, ending the prologue.

OYA.
(Sharp breath out.)
Ah!
AUNT ELEGUA.
I don't know all …
MAMA MOJA.
Nobody does.
AUNT ELEGUA.
But say she ain't even scream.
OYA.
Oya in the air Oya …
SHUN.
Say it sound like the wind …
MAMA MOJA.
Like a breeze …
OYA.
A breeze over Oya.
SHUN.
That's what they say?
ALL.
Huh.
OYA.
Oya … Oya …
AUNT ELEGUA.
She enters.
OYA.
Oya.
MAMA MOJA.
Holding her head.
OYA.
Oya gal …
SHUN.
Laying up somewhere.
MAMA MOJA.
Staring out somewhere.
MAMA MOJA, AUNT ELEGUA, and SHUN.
Somewhere …
ALL.
Huh.

MAMA MOJA.
    Lord God …
OYA.
    Oya …
SHUN.
    That girl
OYA.
    Oya.
AUNT ELEGUA.
    Sweet smiling
OYA.
    Oya in the air …
MAMA MOJA.
    Sad in the eyes
OYA.
    In the air … Oya.
AUNT ELEGUA.
    That's what they say.
SHUN.
    That's what I know …
OYA.
    Oya.
AUNT ELEGUA.
    Beautiful girl.

Scene 1

MAMA MOJA.
    Mama Moja enters the space …
    Where you going Oya?
OYA.
    Gotta go. Track meet.
MAMA MOJA.
    No.
OYA.
    No?

MAMA MOJA.
>Moja looks at Oya like, "What I say?"
>What I say?

OYA.
>Mama I ... You ...
>What you mean?

MAMA MOJA.
>A mother's stare ...

OYA.
>Mama please!

MAMA MOJA.
>I'm tired of you coming in here
>All skin't up from running.
>Running got your body all hurt.

OYA.
>I ain't hurt. I'm fine.
>I just ... I have to run today.

MAMA MOJA.
>You must not be too good
>You come in here all breathin'
>Hard, dirty and funky and all,
>Ankles all swollen. You a good
>Runner?

OYA.
>Yes Mama.

MAMA MOJA.
>You sure?

OYA.
>Yeah I'm sure!

MAMA MOJA.
>Oh yeah? That's what they say, huh?

OYA.
>That's right. I know you heard.
>I'm Oya.

MAMA MOJA.
>Laughing! UH-HUH!
>I know that's right!
>Now that's what I wanna hear!
>You gone out there and show them
>Girls how to.

OYA.

Oya laughs at her crazy mama.

You crazy.

MAMA MOJA.

You my favorite Oya Jean Fair.

OYA.

I'm your only Mama Moja.

MAMA MOJA.

I know that.

Trying to see if you know.

Let me look at you.

OYA.

Here I go.

MAMA MOJA.

They stand for each other.

A reflection ...

OYA.

A face.

BOTH.

Her own.

MAMA MOJA.

(Sharp breath.)

Ah!

Moja's breath comes loose.

She catches her knee.

OYA.

You okay Mama?

MAMA MOJA.

Gone 'head to your meet.

Gone 'head. I be here when you

Get back. Tired just now.

OYA.

You sure Mama?

MAMA MOJA.

Gone. I don't want you missing this one.

Gone.

OYA.

Alright. Oya leaves.

MAMA MOJA.

To run her race.

ELEGBA.
    Enter Li'l 'Legba
    Moja!

Scene 2

MAMA MOJA.
    Not today Lord …
ELEGBA.
    Moja!
MAMA MOJA.
    Loud as hell …
ELEGBA.
    MA MOJA!
MAMA MOJA.
    Moja steps to the porch.
ELEGBA.
    MA …
MAMA MOJA.
    Li'l 'Legba! What I told you 'bout hollerin' fa me huh?
    Screamin' my name like that!
ELEGBA.
    Sorry Moja.
    Where Oya?
MAMA MOJA.
    Runnin' …
ELEGBA.
    Already …
MAMA MOJA.
    Always.
ELEGBA.
    I come to beg some candy or some money to get some.
MAMA MOJA.
    No.
ELEGBA.
    I know it's bad for me, I know it but Mama Moja
    I have to have it, I need it in my life!

MAMA MOJA.
Moja looks at him like "What I say,"
What I say!
ELEGBA.
What I got to do to prove to you I need it?
MAMA MOJA.
You don't need it.
ELEGBA.
What I got to do to prove I gots to have it?
MAMA MOJA.
You can do whatever you please,
Telling me what you gots to have,
I ought to spank your tail!
Send you 'round back to your peoples
So they find out you 'round here begging.
ELEGBA.
They don't mind you giving, Mama Moja.
Sweet Moja. They know you. We love you.
MAMA MOJA.
Moja smiles.
You ain't getting no candy 'Legba.
ELEGBA.
Damn.
MAMA MOJA.
What you say?
ELEGBA.
Somebody say you know dreams.
You understand dreams Mama Moja?
MAMA MOJA.
I mayhap.
ELEGBA.
Sometimes I come home from the schoolhouse tired …
MAMA MOJA.
Uh, Li'l 'Legba …
ELEGBA.
Fall asleep …
I dream with messages I can't read yet …
Need some help with.
I know they messages, just don't know who they to,
Where they from, how to get them there.

MAMA MOJA.
>Moja sighs. Giving into the li'l fucker …
>What your dreams say Li'l 'Legba?

ELEGBA.
>I don't know that's what I'm asking you.

MAMA MOJA.
>Go on Li'l 'Legba …

ELEGBA.
>They hurt now these dreams …

MAMA MOJA.
>Tell me your dreams li'l boy!
>Mumbling to herself,
>Shitc'monIain'tgotalldayforthisfoolishness.
>Sorry Lord.

ELEGBA.
>It's always about the water, my dreams.
>Near it or around it. Sometimes I stand
>In the high tide and I can't breathe but I
>Can breathe. And I walk on the bottom on
>The floor of the waters and they's these people
>Walk alongside me but they all bones and they
>Click the bone people, they talk in the click.
>I say, "Where y'all going" and they say, "Just
>Walking for a while," I say, "Don't you want
>To go home … " They say, "When we walk there, it
>Wasn't there no more." I feel bad for them …
>Then they click and I come up on the mud part,
>Like they send me to the land part, and I'm
>Sitting there waiting 'cause I know they want
>Me to wait I wait there looking and on
>Top of the waters is Oya …
>Li'l 'Legba looks for Moja's reaction.

MAMA MOJA.

ELEGBA.
>Oya girl floating on top of the water,
>Looking up towards the sky and with no clothes
>She hardly got no clothes on and she got her legs
>wide …
>Li'l 'Legba ducks …

14

MAMA MOJA.

ELEGBA.
    And she holding her head on the side with her
    hand like something ailing her.
    But from her legs blood coming down and it's making the
    pond
    red ...
    All the water around her red but she
    Ain't in pain Mama Moja she ain't in
    no pain it look like just laying on top of
    that water. Brown skin in the red water
    and I stick my hand in the water to make
    it wavy so she see me on the land I want
    to ask her something but she don't look
    at me so I stick my hand in the water to make
    it shake her on top and the water comes back in
    a wave, that red and brown water, wash on me
    and I wake up sweating on my face and wet
    low down, like that water, between my legs, wet ...
MAMA MOJA.
    Mama Moja moves to slap his li'l fresh face.
ELEGBA.
    UHUHYOUTOLDMETOTELLYOU!
MAMA MOJA.
    Moja standing, can't help rehearing
    All that Li'l 'Legba said ...
    Gone, 'Legba, watch Oya run for me.
ELEGBA.
    What it mean Moja?
    What my dream mean?
MAMA MOJA.
    Mama Moja looks to the sky.
    It mean you becoming a man Li'l 'Legba,
    My Oya a woman and I'm ...
    I'm tired just now.
ELEGBA.
    Li'l 'Legba begins to walk away like the half moon
    In the morning.

Scene 3

THE MEN.
(Chanting.)
EGUNGUN.
   RUN!
      O LI ROON.
      RUN!
             SHANGO.
             RUN
                    OGUN.
                    RUN

EGUNGUN.
   RUN
         O LI ROON.
         RUN
             SHANGO.
             RUN

EGUNGUN.
   RUN
         O LI ROON.
         RUN
             SHANGO.
             RUN
                    OGUN.
                    RUN
                    (Sharp breath out.)
                    AH!

(They continue.)
NIA.
   Look at her!
SHUN.
   Running
AUNT ELEGUA.
   Gone 'head Oya!
SHUN.
   Running

NIA.

Her powerful legs …

SHUN.

Running

AUNT ELEGUA.

Pressing that ground!

NIA.

Burning it up!

AUNT ELEGUA.

Yes she is …

NIA and AUNT ELEGUA.

Yeah she is!

SHUN.

Running

NIA.

Faster!

AUNT ELEGUA.

Then faster!

NIA.

You can barely see where her feet meet the earth.

AUNT ELEGUA.

Uh-uh barely see where they meet.

NIA.

Gone around that track!

SHUN.

Running

NIA.

Just love to watch her.

SHUN.

Huh

Running like that.

AUNT ELEGUA.

Gone 'head girl!

(The men stop chanting.)

ALL THE WOMEN.

She won!

ALL.

YEAH!

NIA.

They all go forward to hug and congratulate.

THE MAN FROM STATE.
(Or O Li Roon.)
> When The Man From State cuts in front of everyone.
> Oya girl you are blessed … Did you see how them
> other girls couldn't even keep up with you? They just
> Stop running after while and just look at your
> legs flying around, flying through the air.
> The white man lifts his hat so you could see his eyes,
> Oya gal you got a mean run on you.

OYA.
> Thank you.
> Kind of you.

THE MAN FROM STATE.
> Oya gal you come run for me like that? We
> Love to have you at state, love for you to
> Bring in us some championships, I ain't
> Gone lie to you Oya gal we ain't got
> Much in the way of offerin' but you
> Come be one in our school, come be one of
> Our number as it were and we treat you
> Right … we treat you good.

OYA.
> I … don't know sir I
> Wish I could answer now but I gotta
> talk to my mama.

THE MAN FROM STATE.
> Well tell her what I
> said. See what she say. Get back to me …
> But come on quick Oya gal. That spot in
> the sun ain't shining eternal.

OYA.
> Oya breathes and smiles.

OGUN.
> That beautiful smile.

SHANGO.
> But she was bleeding.

ELEGBA.
> Everyone saw it.

OGUN.
> How could they not?

18

OYA.
Oh I …
(The men all step towards Oya, the women block them out.)
I … I just …
SHUN.
Didn't you know it was coming?
OYA.
Well I … I mean … 'cause of the running …
It gets off and …
SHUN.
Huh.
NIA.
She didn't know.
AUNT ELEGUA.
Oya …
SHUN.
Stupid girl.

Scene 4

OGUN.
Ogun Size on Oya's front porch.
F-F-Fine runnin' out there.
OYA.
Hey Ogun, how you doin'?
OGUN.
So, so beautiful …
I mean to, to see you …
I mean to, to see you run like that
So beautiful.
Make me almost wanna fall asleep.
OYA.

OGUN.
I mean, not 'cause I'm … No because you, it's
It's, it's got this song to it your legs like
A crickets, but more beautiful but still when

19

                They
                Ogun moves his fingers like legs runnin',
                When they move like this they start stir, stirring
                A song in the air … like, like a li'l lull aby … sing-singing to
                me softly. Move so so
                Fast they start to sing. You know?
                In the a-air O, Oya in the air.
OYA.
                Oya sad, smiles.
OGUN.
                What's wrong?
OYA.
                You hurt my heart. When you stutter like that.
OGUN.
                I … I do that! I don't …
                Giving effort to not stutter,
                Mean it Oya.
OYA.
                I know. It's like I know you … What you want to say and
                sometimes when it halts up like that
                when the words get stuck in your chest, when they could
                come out so sweet I just … I get sad for you … that's all.
OGUN.
                Oya I … I … I …
SHANGO.
                Enter Shango.
                What up, Ogun?
OGUN.
                He-Hey …
SHANGO.
                C'mon nigga get it out.
OGUN.
                I … Hey Shango.
SHANGO.
                How you doin' man?
                I see you trying to woo the ladies
                Still which yo' half-out words.
OGUN.
                Oh man stop, stop teasing me.

SHANGO.
    Nah I ain't teasing you man …
    You my man Ogun.
OGUN.
    Hey Shango …
SHANGO.
    You think I can talk to Oya here for
    a minute?
OGUN.
    Oh … uh …
SHANGO.
    Shango steps in front of Ogun.
    Thanks man I 'preciate it.
OGUN.
    Ogun leaves the way he came.
SHANGO.
    Oya gal, Oya gal.
    You ran that race.
OYA.
    How you doin' Shango?
SHANGO.
    Oh I'm phyne …
    You know
    Shango laughs
    I'm fine.
OYA.
    That's good.
SHANGO.
    You looked so good out there, girl. So good.
    Running
    Yeah you was.
    'Til you started bleeding but still …
    You know you can't help that.
    Nah. But still damn.
    He adjusts his dick.
    He puts his leg up.
    He licks his lips.
    I rarely look at dark girls like that,
    But you black and phyne.
    So I couldn't help it.

OYA.

Huh.

SHANGO.

Nah don't get all like that.

Why dark women always

got to get mad so quick?

OYA.

We can't change color, like the yellow girls when they blush

so we get mad quick so you can see it in our face.

SHANGO.

You crazy girl. Why you so crazy?

You smell good. Oya how you been running all

day and still smell good.

MAMA MOJA.

(Offstage.)

'Cause I teach Her to wash every day

Enter Mama Moja.

And not to play with trash ...

I say Oya gal,

Moja moves in

Don't play with trash, hear,

it gets in yah eyes, baby,

it gets in yah eyes.

SHANGO.

Oh how you doin' Ms. Moja.

MAMA MOJA.

Evening come Shango.

Yo' mama missing her third-born.

When the rent time come she don't pay

No portion of it for over here ...

Think you need to enjoy what she pay for.

Think you need to be where she prepare a place for you.

SHANGO.

You have a good night, Oya,

Exit Shango.

MAMA MOJA.

Some of the nastiest things come wrapped like that ...

OYA.

He alright Mama don't mix words on him,

he just smelling himself.

MAMA MOJA.

The scent strong ... You sure you don't smell him too?

OYA.

Mama!

MAMA MOJA.

Boys start smelling and those that was ladies and gentlemen
Something start coming away and they get back to animals
again
Sniffin' each other.

OYA.

He gone Mama, Shango just silly like boys get.
Mama.

MAMA MOJA.

Moja, not listening, folds a little.
Uh.

OYA.

Mama!

MAMA MOJA.

Moja holds out her hand and waves Oya back.
Just tired.
Take me inside please.

Scene 5

THE MAN FROM STATE.

(Or O Li Roon.)

The Man From State stands

OYA.

Oya looks out forward. Head high.
I don't know how to say this sir. Yes I
Do. First I say thank you, sir, very much I
Wish I could come on with you this year I do.
I love to run. Nobody loving kicking
Up dirt on a track like me. That I know,
That I feel. But I love my mama. And
She been low lately. Low. She say she ain't
Got long. I don't believe her but I do.

23

And sir you don't know but I'd be lying
If I say I wouldn't go crazy if something
Happened to Moja while I was away.
She say just a year, this year. I stay
With her this while. I will that's what I will do.
But I'll keep training keeping running, always
Running. I know there might not be a chance
Next year but there might be. But there may not be
Moja when I got back … So I'ma stay here. To
See her stay or … go. Thank you so much sir.
Have a good year.

Scene 6

OYA.
> It was late one night,
> Early one morning …
> Ah!
> Oya wakes from a dream.

MAMA MOJA.
> Moja stands in the early
> Morning dew, her hair down,
> Standing, staring from her porch.

OYA.
> Oya finds her there.

MAMA MOJA.
> Moja
> Listening. Somewhere …
> In the distance,

OYA.
> Near distance …

MAMA MOJA.
> She can hear ol' Death calling.

OYA.
> Mama.

AUNT ELEGUA.
> *Gonna lay down my burdens,*

MAMA MOJA.
> Moja throws her hand at Oya.

AUNT ELEGUA.
> *Down by the riverside*

OYA.
> Telling her to stay back.

AUNT ELEGUA.
> *Down by the riverside*

MAMA MOJA.
> Stay back.

AUNT ELEGUA.
> *Down by the riverside*

MAMA MOJA.
> Mama Moja moves
> To lay her cross down.

OYA.
> Oya sees it.

MAMA MOJA.
> How could she not?

OYA.
> Mama?
> You hear me calling to you.
> Listen to me. Like the wind calling you Mama.

(Mama Moja begins walking a path led by Aunt Elegua. Oya tries to follow.)

OYA.
> Mama!
> Where you going?!

MAMA MOJA.
> Oya, in the air … Oya.
> Go on back Oya.
> This between me and the Lord.
> Gone back. You can't follow.

OYA.
> But you can stay … Hear Mama?
> I can't follow but you can stay
> You know that now. Stay Mama Moja.

MAMA MOJA.
    Not now, no.

OYA and MAMA MOJA.
    Not now.
MAMA MOJA.
    Gone 'head to run your race.
AUNT ELEGUA.
    I ain't gonna study war no more,
    Ain't gonna study war no more.
SHUN and AUNT ELEGUA.
    I ain't gonna study war no more,
    I ain't gonna study war no more.
    Ain't gonna study war no more.
OYA.
    And with tears in her eyes.
MAMA MOJA.
    Tremors in her body.
OYA.
    Oya watches her mother …
MAMA MOJA.
    Leave this world.
(Aunt Elegua waves her hand.)
    Mama Moja lets out a sharp breath,
MAMA MOJA.
    Ah!
(She collapses.)
OYA.
    Oya begins to
    Weep for her mother.
ELEGBA.
    Enter Li'l 'Legba, weeping!

Scene 7

OYA.
    Oh Lord!

ELEGBA.
    It ain't right, it ain't right!

OYA.
    Why is he so loud?
    'Legba what's wrong?

ELEGBA.
    Yo' Mama's dead!

OYA.
    Li'l 'Legba it's okay. I know …
    Trying to comfort him and herself …
    She ain't in no more pain!

ELEGBA.
    What make you think I'm crying for her?

OYA.
    You say … I say Li'l 'Legba why you …

ELEGBA.
    Nah you didn't you say "Li'l 'Legba what's wrong … "
    I tell you. I say yo' mama dead that's what wrong with me
    I ain't crying for Moja what my tears do for her.

OYA.
    Not wanting to deal.
    Alright now, look.

ELEGBA.
    Eh I am in grief damnit!
    Thinking.
    You wanna grief with me?

OYA.
    No Li'l 'Legba …

ELEGBA.
    What you too good to grief and wail with me?
    C'mon woe the while.

OYA.
    Li'l boy!

ELEGBA.

'Legba, my name 'Legba …

OYA.

I know who you …

ELEGBA.

'Legba cries.

OYA.

Li'l 'Legba!

ELEGBA.

Oh it ain't right this world sometimes!

OYA.

No … No it isn't.

ELEGBA.

Dead Mama Moja, dead. Who will give me li'l candies
when I come by and say hi?

OYA.

'Legba c'mon now. I will give you …

ELEGBA.

'Legba stops crying.

Look now … I am griefin' and moanin', alright?

Go on in the house if you gone do all that talking.

Some people ain't got no respect … 'Legba moans

SHANGO.

Enter Shango.

Hey Oya girl …

OYA.

Shango.

SHANGO.

I'm sorry 'bout her passin.

OYA.

Thank you.

SHANGO.

That always sound funny to me …

Somebody die and you say sorry and they say thank you
never sound right to me

OYA.

It don't sound right to me either.

You got something more clever for me to say?

SHANGO.

Nah I ain't accusing you of nothing …

I said it too when my daddy died
But it never felt right you know?
Never felt right.

OYA.
Oya girl looks to the sky.
Finds no answer there.

SHANGO.
She breathes like the wind.

ELEGBA.
'Legba sneaks off opposite of how he come.

SHANGO.
You look like you stand some company.

OYA.
Li'l 'Legba is here ...

SHANGO.
Li'l 'Legba?

OYA.
Nothing.

SHANGO.
I know I been ...
In the past I ain't been right ...

OYA.
You got to be you.

SHANGO.
That's what I say. Always be you, and ...
People fit together different.
I fit with you different than I fit with other people
I got something drawing to you and I feel you drawing to me.
Shango curls his fingers around Oya's ear and caresses the soft.

OYA.
Huh.

SHANGO.
So I'm lying? You don't feel nothing for me?

OYA.
I ain't say all that.

SHANGO.
But then ... I mean it ain't love ...
'Cause if it was love it would easily turn
hate how much I get on your nerves.

OYA.

That you do.

SHANGO.

You get on my nerves too.

OYA.

Huh.

SHANGO.

But I think I adore you.

OYA.

Oya takes a breath …

SHANGO.

Tasting Shango's drift.

I like you getting on my nerves

Sometimes.

OYA.

Sometimes.

SHANGO.

I'm alright with that.

I like you most of the time …

'cept you be acting all dark-skinned.

OYA.

See …

Niggas.

You was doing good.

SHANGO.

I'm still here, I still doing alright.

OYA.

'Cause my mama ain't here to run you off.

SHANGO.

You know that ain't right. You know she always here.

And even if she ain't here, she there

Shango points to Oya's heart

and here to …

He points to his own.

OYA.

Oya breathes.

SHANGO.

Like the wind.

Let me take you inside.

OYA.

I don't ... don't need you to do that.

SHANGO.

I didn't say I got to take you inside I asked you to let me ...
Shango offers his hand.

OYA.

Oya sees it.

SHANGO.

How could she not?

OYA.

They go in ...

BOTH.

Together.

Scene 8

SHANGO.

WHAT!

OYA.

YOU HEARD ME!

SHANGO and OYA.

SHANGO AND OYA.

OYA.

FROM INSIDE!

SHANGO.

YELLING SO LOUD!

SHUN.

THIS EARLY IN THE MORNING!

NIA.

OKAY, WAKING UP ALL THE PROJECTS!

SHANGO.·

Damn it Oya!

OYA.

Don't cuss me in my house ...

SHANGO.

Eh fuck yo' house ...
It's too early for all this.

31

OYA.

>Why did you bring it then?

SHANGO.

>I ain't start this thunder!
>I ain't even get up with the devil this morning!
>I just said don't be all hugged up on me.

OYA.

>This is my house, you sleeping in my bed, next to me!
>If I can't be all up on you in my house in my bed
>Where can I do it then, show me!

SHANGO.

>I done told you.
>I don't want nobody all up on me
>When I'm sleep …
>That's what the fuck I said …
>I know I ain't stutter,
>That ain't what I do …
>Shit.

OYA.

>Coming outside.
>Niggas!

AUNT ELEGUA.

>Aunt Elegua coming down the street
>Oya gal …
>Weeping.
>Oya gal!
>Moaning.
>Yo' mama dead and gone!
>Come let your Aunt Ele' love you.

OYA.

>Hey Aunt Elegua?

AUNT ELEGUA.

>I don't know what I am gone do!
>Yo' mama's dead and gone.

OYA.

>She been dead for months …

AUNT ELEGUA.

>Elegua stops and looks at her smart-ass
>Goddaughter.
>Huh.

She breaks down again.
And I still ain't figured out what to do …
You need someone to watch over you!

OYA.

I'm fine Aunt Elegua.

AUNT ELEGUA.

Me and Moja was close.
Like a sister and now that she gone
I say to myself last night I say self that girl over there
lonely …

OYA.

I ain't been lonely.

AUNT ELEGUA.

In that house without no one to talk to …

OYA.

I'm fine.

AUNT ELEGUA.

And here I am call myself a friend to Moja and —

SHANGO.

Enter Shango …

AUNT ELEGUA.

Who this?

OYA.

Shango this Elegua.

AUNT ELEGUA.

Huh.
Yousa phyne thang ain't you.
Yes sir looka here looka here.
This here your friend Oya girl?

OYA.

Yes Shango is my friend.

AUNT ELEGUA.

Y'all lovers and friends?

OYA.

Aunt Ele'!

AUNT ELEGUA.

Oh honey I'm just asking ain't judging
nah nah. Just asking. I wouldn't mind if I do …

SHANGO.

Do what?

OYA.

    Huh.

AUNT ELEGUA.

    Nah girl I was just being silly.

    You sleep here Shango baby?

SHANGO.

    Sometimes when Oya don't make me go home …

OYA.

    Ey!

AUNT ELEGUA.

    Yeah girl I figured that's how you did it.

OYA.

    Aunt Elegua …

AUNT ELEGUA.

    Stop all that … umming and ahing
    standing like you got to pee, honey
    you don't need to dance for me
    I know the story, I ain't your mama
    you ain't got to 'splain nothing to me.
    So y'all sweet strong on each other or
    this a bitter honeysuckle y'all sipping on.
    Who got which in they mouth?

OYA.

    We just friends Aunt Ele' …

AUNT ELEGUA.

    I ain't meddlin' in your business.
    I ain't. I got my own business to take care of
    wondering if yo' mama left me anything in the house.
    Something for me?

OYA.

    There's a box of things I know she would have wanted you to have.

AUNT ELEGUA.

    Thank you girl.
    Gone head and get it,
    I'll keep an eye on God's heaven for you.

OYA.

    Oya exits.

AUNT ELEGUA.

    You ever been with a older woman?

SHANGO.

    Ain't none of 'em like that Oya.

AUNT ELEGUA.

    You stepping out on my god-baby!

SHANGO.

    She kicks me out.

    Sometimes we can't stand the sight of each other …

AUNT ELEGUA.

    But when you make up …

SHANGO.

    It's all in the making up.

AUNT ELEGUA.

    How she like you to make up to her?

SHANGO.

    Like all women do …

    On my knees.

OYA.

    Oya returns.

AUNT ELEGUA.

    What you doing now, Oya,

    With this freak here?

    This boy got a wickedness in his

    Stance, a driving in his pants

    What a good girl doing with somebody like him …

OYA.

    I ask the same question.

AUNT ELEGUA.

    You ain't trying to get my baby pregnant is you.

SHANGO.

    Hell nah! You crazy?

OYA.

    Hell nah? Why you actin' like that?

SHANGO.

    I ain't trying to have no youngin' makin' me grown …

AUNT ELEGUA.

    What you care? You trying to get pregnant?

    Eh you can't run pregnant Oya.

    You still running that man say come on in

    A year … You ready?

OYA.

Yeah Aunt Elegua, I'm running.

SHANGO.

To Oya,

Lying.

AUNT ELEGUA.

Don't you think it's 'bout time to show him you still got it

Fall coming ain't it …

OYA.

It's just spring.

AUNT ELEGUA.

You giving me mouth Oya gal,

It ain't saying what it should!

You better listen Ele' when she talk yeah!

You better come on now.

Get your nose out that boy and what?

OYA.

Get your mind right.

AUNT ELEGUA.

There it is. I know you ain't forgot.

Get your books when?

OYA.

First.

AUNT ELEGUA.

Get some dick when?

OYA.

Later.

AUNT ELEGUA.

That's right be fast in the feet and not in the ass.

C'mon on now. Listen to Ele'.

Call up that man get him to see you can

run like Oya gal so he can step you up.

This asphalt still be burning hot when you get back.

SHANGO.

You know that huh?

AUNT ELEGUA.

If it ain't one black road work it's another.

OYA.

Oya smiles.

ELEGBA.
    A li'l older 'Legba enters
    breathing hard laughing breathing.

Scene 9

SHANGO.
    Exit Shango.
O LI ROON.
    O Li Roon enters mad as hell.
    Y'all better get him, hear!
    Catch him before I do! Because if I lay hands
    On Elegba ... I swear 'fore God!
OYA.
What you rushing over here screaming for O Li Roon?
O LI ROON.
    Didn't I tell you, didn't I tell you, if you stole from me
    again 'Legba I was gone burn you, do something to you
    Like they do cross the waters, in K'wait burn your booty hair
    something
    So you know damnit why don't you learn? So hard-headed!
    COME HERE!
ELEGBA.
    'Legba laughing.
    Running ducking.
    Get off me!
OYA.
What you stealin for 'Legba!
ELEGBA.
    Went in his store told him I want some Candy.
    He say gone and get the chocolate 'Legba it's right there.
OYA.
    So you took it?
ELEGBA.
    I say I ain't got no money nah.
O LI ROON.
    And I say then you don't want no chocolate!

ELEGBA.
And I say that's a boldfaced lie bitch!
OYA.
'Legba!
ELEGBA.
I still want chocolate whether I got the money for it
or not ... I still want it. He gone talk 'bout ...
nigga tell him what you said you standing right there!
O LI ROON.
Let me catch hold of him,
I won't turn him loose!
Lord swear!
OYA.
O Li Roon don't argue with that boy.
O LI ROON.
You know that ain't no boy
this li'l motherfucker been here before!
ELEGBA.
You the stupidest white man I done seen!
How I been here before and I'm standing in front of you!
If I been here, you been here too
and you ought to be smart enough to know better than to test me!
O LI ROON.
I ain't test you,
I say Li'l 'Legba you don't want that
candy man unless you got the money for it.
ELEGBA.
And I shook for you.
Hell I stood on my hands to show
You ... Emptied my pockets out and out onto the floor,
Let the li'l balls of inside pocket fall out to
Demonstrate for yo' half-cocked eye ass
That I ain't had the money and wasn't gone get it soon
But that I was still salivating for that candy.
How you gone tell me what I want and don't want?
I can't stand fo nobody to tell me what I feel ain't
really there ... I said how much you wanna bet I want that candy!
O LI ROON.
And I got wise to that shit
'cause the last time you brought your black ass in my store.

AUNT ELEGUA.
Hold on Li …
O LI ROON.
Oh what he ain't black?
What y'all catching breath 'cause I called him what he is
I was raised here too. Right on the bayou.
Yo' mamas beat my ass with you when you got in trouble …
His ass is black and mine is white
His lying black ass talking about some, "I bet cha a dollar I
want that candy."
I say, "I ain't betting"
'Cause last time he took the candy and ate it through the
wrapper, like he crazy.
Talking 'bout, "See there, see how much I want it. That prove
it. I eat it through the wrapper. Just like eating pussy. I eat it
through the panties to get it."
OYA.
Oya trying not to laugh
You so nasty.
ELEGBA.
'Legba licks his lips.
O LI ROON.
I made his li'l ass get out my store talking like that nasty.
That time I just made him leave the store. But here 'Legba
again in my face talking about some candy. You the candy-
talkingness punk I know! I said go get the money for it …
Here he go … "Oh okay" looking like a motherless child.
Long-ass arms swinging sad like a sweet chariot. I started
to give him the candy but then he gon' snatch the goodie
and run.
OYA.
You left to run after fifty cents worth a candy?
You got a whole store full of merchandise
AUNT ELEGUA.
And got a handful of hoodlums outside it.
OYA.
You locked the door behind you Li?
ELEGBA.
Hell nah …

AUNT ELEGUA.
>You gone be missing more than fifty cent
>you come back honey.

OYA.
>Here go your fifty cent Li go back to the store ...

O LI ROON.
>You so sweet, so sweet. Looking after *this* mischief,
>Caring for people around you. So good
>To everybody Oya. Remember you
>Remember you watch my daughter, my
>Baby girl you remember?

OYA.
>Yeah Li I do.

O LI ROON.
>She remember you Oya. You only watch her
>One time but she always say to me, "Pa
>Li Roon when Ms. Mama Oya come watch
>Me again?" You believe that? She call you Ms.
>Mama Oya!

OYA.
>Huh.
>Oya smiles.
>Huh.

ELEGBA.
>You still owe me fifty cent.

O LI ROON.
>Oh I got the whole G-unit for you
>Li Roon jumps to get 'Legba

OYA.
>Gone Li.

O LI ROON.
>O Li Roon exits.

AUNT ELEGUA.
>Who li'l boy this is?

ELEGBA.
>Who big woman you is?

AUNT ELEGUA.
>Alright now you got slick with the white man
>I beat the snot out your ass and tell yo' mama!
>Elegua smiles.

I like him! He full of something. Like light ...
You got pretty eyes boy. Who you leading
With them eyes? You gone be my husband
When you get grown. I promise you.
ELEGBA.
You e'er break promises?
AUNT ELEGUA.
Nope.
ELEGBA.
I ain't neva growing up,
y'all be on suicide watch tomorrow.
AUNT ELEGUA.
Oh he full of it ...
Just life and mischief.
Sing us a song.
ELEGBA.
This ain't no show!
AUNT ELEGUA.
Oh nigga shut up and sing.
Shit you sit 'round here with all that mouth
now somebody tell you to open it
and you shy between the teeth?
Get you ass over here sing for Aunt Ele' ...
Where did darkness go?
OYA.
Oh, he's gone like he do.
AUNT ELEGUA.
Aw girl, don't worry make him miss something ...
Go 'head, sing.
OYA.
Yeah 'Legba, sing
AUNT ELEGUA.
What your name again baby?
ELEGBA.
Mumblingsothatthefatladycan'thearme.
AUNT ELEGUA.
Mouth!
Thats what I'ma call you
Mouth.
Sing us a song, Mouth!

41

ELEGBA.
    'Legba smiles.
    Lord she big
    Lord see that!
    Lord this lady, all woman
    Born with her own rack of fat back
    Lord she ...
AUNT ELEGUA.
    Elegua is not amused.
    You funny baby. But I know your mama,
    whoe'er she is would love for my fat ass to roll
    'round there and say what?
ELEGBA.
    Mouth was stealing?
AUNT ELEGUA.
    I bet you she would have a song for you.
    You better find some medley in all that mouth.
ELEGBA.
    I got a dream I could sing.
OYA.
    Dream?
AUNT ELEGUA.
    Excited!
    C'mon Mouth woo me boy!
ELEGBA.
    A spell comes o'er 'Legba.
    Hear 'Legba sing
    Sing of her road
    Hear 'Legba cry
    Knowing her load
    Come down peace,
    Come down night
    Cover over Oya girl
    Make her world alright.
AUNT ELEGUA.
    Ah hell nigga I thought
    You was gone busta rhyme
    or something ...
ELEGBA.
    'Legba stares at Elegua.

AUNT ELEGUA.
> Gone head sing yo' li'l song.
> Everybody wanna be an idol …

OYA.
> Oya's breath.

ELEGBA.
> She bleeds now,
> Her wounds all close,
> She breathes still
> But her chest never rose
> Come down peace
> Come down night
> Cover over Oya girl
> Make her world alright.

(He hums.)

Scene 10

THE MAN FROM STATE.
(Or O Li Roon.)
> The Man From State stands …
> Oya girl …

OYA.
> Yes sir.

THE MAN FROM STATE.
> I am sorry Oya gal I really am I
> wished you would have c'mon when
> I asked you too, I do. But you know
> that's a good lesson on this life you
> never can tell what will happen to your
> chances you gotta jump when you can
> move, when you can move, you …
> Young people like … like yourself don't have much
> in the way of opportunity in this world …

OYA.
> Wait sir please …

THE MAN FROM STATE.

I mean I would give you a chance I would
but the top girl we got she man oh man …
When you didn't come to us Oya gal
We had to get a second best; go there on
our list. I don't like second nothing but such
is life, like I told you chance to go, go, you know.
She found she was the second on our list, ooh wee.
Hell I didn't mince no words bout it I told her square
I say, "You our second. Gotta girl named Oya run
like the wind. She say she coming on in a year."

OYA.

Sir …

THE MAN FROM STATE.

That girl found out she was our second, Oya and you would
be surprised what people do to get to th' top some.
This here girl said to herself, I reckon, she show us good and
plenty. That we wouldn't wanna look nowhere else when we
see what she can do. Took about seven off her time …
just like that. Every time since she stepped on our grassy?
she been running for her life look like.
Seven consistent. Seven like that … and then more.
I never seen nothing like it in m'life.
Never.
I do hope you keep training there Oya.
And you know keep yourself up …
But we just ain't got no place for you here.
No, not here.

OYA.

Oya sad, smiles.
Taking it in.

ELEGBA.

(Hums.)

Scene 11

SHANGO.
   Enter Shango, dressed in an Army recruit uniform.
ELEGBA.
(Hums.)
OYA.
   What you come to tell me dressed like that?
   We ... we through? That's what you saying?

SHANGO.

OYA.
   Nothing to say? Huh.
   All the years I know'd you got mouth to say
   what come to it. Now what? Speechless?
ELEGBA.
(Hums.)
OYA.
   Shango just speak your words and I'll be free.
   Free from you coming, tasting me at night,
   Me smelling you smelling like somebody else
   Yeah say it, unspell me Shango. Do me a favor.
   That's what you gone say right? That's what you doing me a
   ...
SHANGO.
   Shango moves to ...
OYA.
   No!
SHANGO.

OYA.
   I ain't going to school no more ...
   I, they ain't got no place for me.
   Nowhere for me to go but here, I'm here.
   I can't go nowhere. Just be here.
   Here.

SHANGO.
>Shango curls his fingers around Oya's ear
>And caresses.

OYA.

SHANGO.
>Exit Shango.

ELEGBA.
>*(Hums.)*

OYA.
>Oya's breath comes hard to her.

AUNT ELEGUA.
>They say she broke down ...

SHUN.
>That's what they say.

MAMA MOJA.
>Or that she broke a spell.

SHUN.
>Broke something.

AUNT ELEGUA.
>Something happened.

ALL THE WOMEN.
>Something.

ELEGBA.
>Come down peace,
>Come down night
>Cover over Oya girl
>Make her world alright.
>Li'l 'Legba exits like
>a three-quarter moon in the morning.

(Oya stares out.)

Scene 12

OGUN.
>Enter Ogun Size
>I ... I ... know ... I know that that you can he-hear me,

S-So I'm I'm just stand ing here talking.
Standing h-here speaking to you, my h-heart.
Y ... You don't know ... You s-so blind
If you as-ask me.
I ain't n-never said nothing
like that to you b but how you think it make m-me make me
... You ain't neva let me love you, but you gone lay down
and get closer to death? Snuggle up to him!
Death with his stale breath don't know you like I do.
He just a nasty ole man been looking at you since you was
was a li'l girl. But I been loving you always.
I been in love with your light and your sad eyes.
And I got this home inside me I know I do ...
My outside seem like it's fragile but in here
a big man that will wrap you in love, Oya.
You come home with Ogun. Just come home.
You let me take care of you for a while.
I'll make it alright. I'll make it okay.

OYA.
Oya stops her staring and looks at him.
You're not stuttering.

OGUN.
What?
Laughing.

OYA.
You not stuttering.

OGUN.
How you feeling?
I should c-call somebody ...

OYA.
No!
Don't start again.
Don't start stuttering just talk to me.

OGUN.
For the rest of my life.

OYA.

OGUN.
I won't skip another word. Another breath
won't interrupt myself, you let me talk to you.

47

Oya in the air, Oya.
Let's go inside. We can talk quiet in there.
Come inside with me. We talk about starting
Something. Making a family one day …
OYA.
Oya smiles.
(The cast hums the opening. Ogun and Oya join them in the pantheon upstage. Lights.)

End of Act One

ACT TWO

Scene 1

Lights.

Shun and Nia dance downstage.

Oya sits on her porch.

Music plays.

THE OJAYS.
  I love music!
SHUN and NIA.
  Ah!
  Ah!
  Ah!
SHUN.
  A party nearby!
NIA.
  Going loud!
SHUN.
  Music!
NIA.
  Dancing!
SHUN and NIA.
  A baby shower!
  Ah!
  I love music …
  Any kind of music!
  Hey!
OYA.
  Oya sitting on her porch,
  Staring at the shower.

Look at Sophie dancing like that.
Look how big her belly is ...
Lord.
Oya staring.
She must be so happy.
(Music changes. A song like "Thank You for My Child" by Cheryl Pepsi Riley. *)
NIA.
Ooh girl!
SHUN.
This is my song!
OYA.
Oya on her porch.
I hate this song.
OGUN.
Ogun Size enters ready for work
This a nice song.
Better than all that noise they've been playing all night.
OYA.
It's too early to go to the car shop.
OGUN.
The early bird catches the worm.
OYA.

OGUN.
Oya, don't sit here all night and morning.
OYA.
I shouldn't let you walk out there
Make you go lay down.
So I can come in later listen to you snore.
OGUN.
I don't snore.
OYA.
You breathe hard.
OGUN.
I breathe hard ...
OYA.

OGUN.

    You so sweet.

OYA.

    Gone Ogun.

OGUN.

    So sweet but you can't taste your sugar.

    Ogun kiss.

    I gotta go, gotta go.

    Ogun kiss

    See you later

    Ogun kiss

    Bye baby

    Kiss

OYA.

    Don't be all up on me!

OGUN.

    See you later baby.

OYA.

    Music from the shower still going ...

OGUN.

    We'll play good music at your shower one day.

OYA.

    One day.

OGUN.

OYA.

OGUN.

    Don't sit out there all night, Oya.

OYA.

OGUN.

    Ogun Size exits to work.

(Music from the party stops.)

ELEGBA.

    'Legba sneaks in like the moon.

OYA.

    Oya bows her head.

ELEGBA.

    'Legba hums

OYA.
>   Boy …
>   Why you always sneaking?

ELEGBA.
>   I'm not sneaking,
>   I'm watching.

OYA.
>   You getting too big to be doing that.
>   Watching me. I know those looks …

ELEGBA.
>   I can't do nothing with them.

OYA.
>   People talk about those looks 'Legba.
>   People talk 'bout you 'Legba.

ELEGBA.
>   So you heard?

OYA.
>   Who ain't heard about you getting kicked out,
>   Your mama putting you out?

ELEGBA.
>   I'm a man now Oya.

OYA.
>   Don't think she ain't gone take you back …

ELEGBA.
>   She say don't be back for nine months.
>   Don't come back till it's born.

OYA.

ELEGBA.

OYA.
>   Who? You got somebody pregnant?

ELEGBA.
>   'Legba beams like the moon.

OYA.
>   'Legba how old is that girl?
>   She my age?

ELEGBA.
>   She ain't no girl.
>   Oba all woman.

OYA.

You always did like older women.

What she doing messing with you?

ELEGBA.

She say I got an old soul.

I say, I'm just sixteen.

She say, "in this lifetime but you really like fifty."

I say, "Yeah right but when I lay you down

you will know why they say boys never stop

playing with they toys."

OYA.

Boy shut up!

Laughing!

So nasty!

ELEGBA.

Never stop playing with they food either.

You know I can eat. I love some chocolate too ...

The older it get, sugar just rise to the top ...

Slurp.

OYA.

See that woman right you

A dirty old man in there.

ELEGBA.

OYA.

ELEGBA.

I can't stop being happy about this.

OYA.

I can't stop smiling at you.

ELEGBA.

We wrong Oya?

It ain't right to be just bringing babies in this world ...

OYA.

What else we got to do? Nothing. Sit around

Watch the world. Babies got some sunshine in em.

I saw some little bow-legged baby

walk 'round here the other day just as cute

I looked at her and I said whose baby is this ...

She looked at me "Not yours," ... She wasn't mean

53

She just say it matter-of-fact and bent down
picked one them firecrackers left from the fourth
I say, li'l baby don't eat that."
She put it right in her mouth and started chewing
like it was this brand-new flavor now and later
just chewing and the burnt orange of the gunpowder
flowing out her mouth … she just smiling.
Her mama walk by and grab up the baby
"What the fuck you got in your mouth"
started spanking her
"Didn't I tell you to not put shit in your mouth … "
The baby start crying. She carrying the baby away looking at
me talking 'bout "And you just gone sit here and let her kill herself"
I wanted to be like "Bitch that ain't my baby"
She just told me I wasn't her mama …
Why she let the baby just roam around the projects
any damn way? As much as they shoot 'round here?
Letting your child just walking around here. Unchecked!

ELEGBA.
'Legba looks at Oya girl.

OYA.
Oya girl feels him staring.
Go in there and get some sleep.
Look like you been up all night.

ELEGBA.
Ogun …

OYA.
He gone to work …
You need to sleep gone head … daddy.

ELEGBA.
Thank you Oya.

OYA.
Uh-huh.

ELEGBA.
'Legba sneaks off like the moon behind a cloud
gone but still there.
(Hums a song like "Call Me" by Aretha Franklin. *)

SHANGO.
Enter Shango dressed in Army fatigues …

---

* See Special Note on Songs and Recordings on copyright page.

OYA.

    Oya's breath.

SHANGO.

    Shango stands in a better light.

OYA.

    A sad song plays ...

SHANGO.

    Sad like when you were little.

OYA.

    Sad like a mother's heartbreak.

SHANGO and OYA.

    Sad ...

SHANGO.

    I saw 'Legba go in.
    What he doing here?

OYA.

    Minding his business ...

SHANGO.

    That li'l boy got business over here?

OYA.

    He ain't that little no more.
    He about to be a daddy.

SHANGO.

    I been gone that long huh?

OYA.

    Long enough.

SHANGO.

    Surprised you ain't swollen up.
    You with somebody I know.

OYA.

    If you know why you asking?

SHANGO.

    Who you been down together in
    your sleep with?

OYA.

    How all of this your business, huh?
    Didn't you just get here?
    Say your hellos to everybody,
    they will tell you all
    the news you wanna know.

I'm not your reporter, seek your
prophecy elsewhere.
SHANGO.
You ought to be swollen, belly full,
glowing with that morning glow ...
Titties perky ready to give life ...
OYA.
I ain't trying to have no youngins making me grown.
Remember that? Please boy. Gone, okay?
Gone Shango.
SHANGO.
Shango curls his fingers ... He caresses ...
You still slim and ripe ...
How somebody ain't put
a baby inside you yet is beyond me.
Exit Shango.

Scene 2

OYA.
Oya
Laughs to herself.
AUNT ELEGUA.
Aunt Ele' sees it,
How could she not?
Ooh Oya gal Oya gal!
Where you coming from smiling like that?
Tell me I love women's secrets!
OYA.
I just came back from ...
AUNT ELEGUA.
He home ain't he?
Shango!
He home from the war or
the crisis ... whatever ...
Your fire is back!
Girl you better go get melted down!

OYA.

    Shhh! Aunt Ele', I'm with Ogun …

AUNT ELEGUA.

    Yeah but he don't walk near you and
    Your temperature change. I have seen you.
    I know what you're like under Ogun Size.
    But it ain't nothing like that lightning
    from Shango, eh?

OYA.

    Aunt Ele'!

AUNT ELEGUA.

    Shango come and he walk over to you
    Your knees clap down, you fall
    On that bed, honey that muscle just
    Grinding on his thigh aching to touch …
    You start to change color you start
    To lose your breath, how they say
    "Huh huh" can you keep up …

OYA.

    Your nephew loves me …
    I love him …

AUNT ELEGUA.

    Something 'bout that say "lie" to me.
    I got to go, I just come thought I be nosy
    Come see if you nosy.
    Come see if your nose wide open.

Scene 3

All the cast, offstage, hums a gospel or spiritual.

OYA.

    Sunday afternoon.
    Oya sitting on her porch.

NIA.

    Nia and Shun walk by.

SHUN.

Laughing to themselves.

NIA.

There go the girl, Shun, almost let Shaunta
kill herself by eating a fireworks. Yeah!
Remember I told you.

SHUN.

Oya Jean Fair almost let my god-baby die, Nia?

OYA.

I told her not to.
She's got a grown li'l mouth.

SHUN.

You should have popped her hand or something.
You grown ain't you?

NIA.

Now you know I would have come 'round
Here and beat Oya ass she would have hit
My baby.

SHUN.

Laughing ...

NIA.

What?

SHUN.

I could just see Shaunta telling
Oya, "You ain't my mama!"

NIA.

Laughing too!
Yeah!
To Oya.
She so bad sometimes ...

SHUN.

Ooh I love her.

OYA.

If she was my baby ...

SHUN.

She ain't your baby you
ain't got no baby.
Don't run out with your mouth.
Tend to your li'l grease monkey.

NIA.

Don't act like that Shun.

Nia and Shun leave.

SHUN.

Laughing.

(All hum "Thank you Lord.")

SHANGO.

Enter Shango.

You weren't at church.

How long it's been since you talk to Jesus?

OYA.

Don't do that.

SHANGO.

I'm just concerned about your soul ...

I wanna see you in the sky when we

all get there.

OYA.

Service still going why you left?

SHANGO.

Ah hell I had to get outta there.

It's going on 4!

First they started late, then the choir ...

OYA.

'Legba was up there?

SHANGO.

I saw him ...

Him and Ogun's brother, Oshoosi.

If I was Ogun I would ship Oshoosi ass

Off to military school ...

Thirteen years old, getting thrown in jail.

OYA.

Oya looks up.

SHANGO.

Yeah, that's why the church going so long.

They praying for his monkey ass.

Choir just up there singing.

Elegua came into the church she mad

As hell. You can tell 'cause her wig all

Tilted to the side and she walking that

Big girl walk towards the altar. She

Talk to the secretary of the mother's board, Mother Pickalo.
Whatever Elegua telling her making her shake and put down
her head.
She starts praying. I'm like what the hell's going on.
Elegua walk up to the choir stand and she just
Start to beating on Oshoosi. Beat beat beat ...
All the way down the aisle of the church and out
The front door. Mother Pickalo, she stands up like she 'bout
to declare war
She standing there you know in the church lady stance
You know with her face fully forward Holy Ghost filled,
double chin jangling. Gone talk about "Giving honor to
God, y'all
I have some news, you know times is hard.
And the devil is out there I know!" People Amen-ing and
yes-Lordin'
I'm like I wish this chick would come the hell on
and stop the testimony ... But you know she crying ...
"And Lord the devil can sometimes sneak in here
too ... This holy sanctuary, Lordie G Lord!
This temple ... this house of God can be sacked with wasteful ...
There was money being stolen from
Out the mouth of God and being used
To play in some corner crap game
Filled with wicked youthful derision. Lord God Lord God.
I ask that this money be prayed over and
Put back into the rightful hands of the church
So it can pay for the pastor's son's gonorrhea of the mouth!"
OYA.
    She didn't say that!
SHANGO.
    How you know you wasn't there?
OYA.
    Elegua came and told me she put Oshoosi in jail for a day ...
SHANGO.
    So you knew this whole time, huh?
    What you let me tell it for?
OYA.
    Wanted you to tell me something.

SHANGO.

He smiles.

OYA.

She smiles ...

SHANGO and OYA.

They ...

SHANGO.

Shango curls ... He caresses ...

ELEGBA

'Legba sneaks in unseen. A bundle in his arms ...

OYA.

Oya smiles.

SHANGO.

You tell me something,

What you doing with Ogun Size?

OYA.

The same thing I was doing with you ...

SHANGO.

He doing it right?

OYA.

Lying.

Every night.

SHANGO.

Like me? Nah not like me.

He eat that pussy like me?

OYA.

You over-steppin' Shango!

SHANGO.

How you mean, I was there first ...

OGUN.

Where you at now Shango?

Enter Ogun Size.

SHANGO.

Shango grins ... A glint of war in his eyes.

"Hi, hi, you doing Ogun ... "

OGUN.

"Oh I'm phyne ... "

You know ...

Ogun laughs in mimic of Shango.

I'm fine.

OYA.
    Oya interrupting
    Gone Shango.
SHANGO.
    Smiling
    I was there first ...
    I'll be there last.
    Exits Shango.
OYA.

OGUN.

OYA.

OGUN.

ELEGBA.
    A baby cries inside.
OYA.
    You hear a baby crying?
OGUN.
    Yeah.
OYA.
    They move to the door ...
OGUN.
    You wanna go in now?
OYA.
    Gone Ogun ...
OGUN.
    You stay outside too much Oya.
    You need stay in sometimes.
    It ain't right for you to be out here all the time.
    One day you'll have something to stay in for.
OYA.
    Let me see what's in my house.
OGUN.
    You should already know.
    You know?
    You should know already.

Scene 4

Shun and Nia stand, and hang clothes on a line.

SHUN.
    Hum.

NIA.
    Huh?

SHUN.
    Hum, so nobody can hear.

NIA.
    Hum

SHUN.
    Sharing a secret.
    Girl 'Legba mama came 'round to Oya house
    Screaming and carrying on!

NIA.
    Laughing,
    Back to humming.
    Hum

SHUN.
    Yeah girl! Cause 'Legba done
    Took his baby and been hiding
    Out at Oya house.

NIA.
    So his mama got the baby now?

SHUN.
    You supposed to be humming?
    I'm supposed to be telling!

NIA.
    Nia hums.
    Hum

SHUN.
    So yeah 'Legba mama got the baby now,
    And she told 'Legba to stay at Oya house.

NIA.

Hum

SHUN.

Oya got a full house,
Cause now Ogun ask
Elegua to stay 'round there!

NIA.

What?

SHUN.

Yeah girl!

NIA.

Nia hums
Hum

SHUN.

The night before Ogun woke up and
saw Oya sitting on the porch rocking … You
remember it was during the blackout
all the power was out in the projects.
Anybody in they right mind be inside
not sitting on they porch but Oya
Say he don't know seem like she losing her mind
Ask Aunt Ele' come and watch her.
But I know the bitch ain't crazy nah
she a li'l hot box and she been getting a visitor.

NIA.

Who?
Hum
Shango!
Hum
But you knew that was coming
I know you ain't mad?

SHUN.

What you talking 'bout Nia!
I ought punch you in your damn face!

NIA.

Ah bitch you jealous you ain't crazy, huh.

SHUN.

Huh.

NIA.

Consoling her friend.

They was together before he left.

SHUN.

I don't care if they was *married* before she stealing
my man now.

NIA.

You know Shango ain't nobody man.

SHUN.

Yet ... You just got to learn how to tether niggas.
Just sing your song Nia.
Don't worry 'bout Shun okay
'Cause when it come to it ...
I know how to run Miss Oya
Where she can't walk.

NIA.

Nia smiles at her friend
She hums.
Hum

Scene 5

OGUN.

Why you let her go?

AUNT ELEGUA.

She grown and got legs
And I asked her to go ...
And further who you think you talking to boy?
I ain't got to 'splain hell of nothing to you!

OGUN.

Aunt Ele' I don't wanna get into it ...

AUNT ELEGUA.

But you step yo' flat foot right in it!

OGUN.

Oya ain't feeling good!

AUNT ELEGUA.

Who you to say that girl ain't feeling good?
She a grown woman ain't she?
Grown enough to know what is and ain't.

OGUN.

    She sitting out, sneaking out all the time.

    Staring got this look on her face.

    She got a sad look on her always …

AUNT ELEGUA.

    Hell life like that …

    You think sadness stop niggas

    From going to the fish market?

OYA.

    Oya enters …

OGUN SIZE.

    Smiling …

AUNT ELEGUA.

    Carrying a bag.

OGUN.

    Let me get that for you.

    Where you been?

OYA.

    Now wait … you just took the bag

    from me.

    Where it look like I been?

OGUN.

    Did you leave outta here carrying that grin?

    Where you pick that up from?

OYA.

    Oya stops smiling

    Nowhere.

OGUN.

    I'm serious … I ain't seen your face like that

    in a long time … Not 'round me.

    I just wanna see it … I …

    I love it …

    I love you.

OYA.

    I gotta help with the fish.

OGUN.

    You know I don't eat fish …

AUNT ELEGUA.

    It's Friday boy …

    Friday the best day for some fish. I never

did understand my sister's kids. Some of
The most finicky eaters. You won't eat fish …
that Oshoosi talking 'bout he can't have no
banana pudding 'cause it make his throat itch.
On top of that neither one of the niggas take in
milks without farting all over the house. Never
understood how y'all get these delicate stomachs
when you starving … seem like to me yo' stomach
be glad to get anything in it. C'mon stay
for some of this fish. You don't eat enough no how.
OGUN.
    Should I stay Oya?
OYA.
    Go on in and lay down 'fore we eat.
OGUN.
    Ogun Size exits hoping to see her smile …
    But only finds a dark cloud in Oya's sky.
OYA.
    Oya looks to Elegua
AUNT ELEGUA.
    I'll start the seasoning …
    Aunt Elegua exits
OYA.
    Oya bows her head.
ELEGBA.
    'Legba tries to sneak in the door with the baby.
OYA.
    'Legba yo' mama say you can't keep the baby 'round here, you
    want her to come here and be mad with all of us.
ELEGBA.
    'Legba smiles at Oya.
    Oya like his sister, Oya.
    He brings the baby to her.
    Eh Oya look here.
    He shows her …
    Straight line of little black marks
    on his leg. See?
    Laughing …
    Like the Lord was trying to send a message on it.
    See it …

OYA.
    Huh …
ELEGBA.
    Hold him …
    'Legba stands back and pulls down his pants …
OYA.
    What you doin'?
ELEGBA.
    'Legba proudly shows Oya his right thigh.
    Same marks. The ones like nobody ever seen
    right here on me and my baby.
    You ever know something yours,
    and from nowhere it proves
    itself, shows itself to be just yours only …
    You ever felt that, Oya?
    Something all yours. This mine.
OYA.
    Oya stares.
ELEGBA.
    When I hold him …
    It's like I got more love in my hands
    Than the world got air to breathe.
    I don't want nothing to keep me from it.
OYA.

ELEGBA.
    I know you understand me.
    Anybody understands me you do.
OYA.
    Sighs.
    Oya gives 'Legba back "more love than the world got air … "
    Oya in the air Oya …
    Go inside 'Legba.
ELEGBA.
    'Legba fades into the house
    like the moon in the shadow of the world.
OYA.
    Oya breaks her spell.
    That's why you named that damn baby Marc!
    You fool!

ELEGBA.
'Legba laughs …
Fades into the house.
OYA.
Oya smiles to herself.
Marc. Huh.
Night. *Come down peace …*
Come down night …
SHANGO.
Enter Shango dressed in his Army fatigues.
Just came to say goodbye.
OYA.
All the nights I've been seeing you
And you just telling me now you leaving?
OGUN.
Ogun Size enters.
SHANGO.
I come to return the reins my man.
OYA.

SHANGO.
I gotta go.
Oya keep your head up.
I tried to leave you a li'l present but …
I gotta go.
Ogun you stay strong man.
Keep your li'l family together.
Exit Shango.
OYA.
Oya curls her fingers behind her ears … she caresses the soft.
Hum

Scene 6

OYA.
Oya in the early evening
Standing on someone else's porch.
She wants to knock on the door but …
She hums.
Hum
THE WOMAN THAT REMINDS YOU.
(Or Mama Moja.)
Don't sing on my doorstep.
A woman of magic, a *bruja*,
A hoodoo voodoo lady walks
To the porch.
OYA.
I got,
my body empty …
THE WOMAN THAT REMINDS YOU.
What you want me to do about it?
OYA.
Please,
I know you know how to fix it.
THE WOMAN THAT REMINDS YOU.
Go to the church ladies that's what they there
For, they all stand over you moaning and praying
They fix you right up.
OYA.
They won't even see I'm in trouble.
They all say you young and you ain't pregnant?
Praise da Lord, bless
the Lord o my soul …
THE WOMAN THAT REMINDS YOU.
God is good …
OYA.
But He is good in all things.
THE WOMAN THAT REMINDS YOU.
Huh. The good God of a thousand and one pieces.

You looking for your piece?

OYA.

You got something, some words,
That make me love right, love where I should.

THE WOMAN THAT REMINDS YOU.

If you ask God of a thousand and one He will provide you
Be careful how you ask it though.
He gives you paths, none of them easy.

OYA.

Then I want my own mark.
I wanna look down and see myself
Mirrored back to me.

THE WOMAN THAT REMINDS YOU.

You should have had that by now.

OYA.

What?

THE WOMAN THAT REMINDS YOU.

You don't think by now you should have
Had something growing inside you?

OYA.

No ... No. I mean not if it wasn't time. Not if it wasn't ...
No!

THE WOMAN THAT REMINDS YOU.

But a grown woman Oya gal?
You been grown for a long time now
How you think it just skipped you?
You ain't been with no little boys.
You had how many, two grown men
From two sides of the world, the fighter
And the business man. Both grown men
And not nar one of 'em filled you with seed
That growed into something? You still walking
'Round here wishing for that? You should know by now ...

OYA.

What I should know?

THE WOMAN THAT REMINDS YOU.

If you ain't got it in your mind I sure as shit ain't gone put it
there.

OYA.

Put something here!

THE WOMAN THAT REMINDS YOU.
>I'm a woman, I can't put nothing there.
>The hoodoo *bruja* goes off her porch.

(Shift.)

OYA.
>Oya turns. Men begin to gather.

O LI ROON.
>Like a rain cloud.

OGUN.
>You may not know …

SHANGO.
>But just like in the middle of the desert …

O LI ROON.
>Out of nowhere comes torrential rain …

EGUNGUN.
>Around here sometimes out of nowhere …

ALL.
>A party.

SHANGO.
>The speakers get setup on one block …

OGUN.
>The music comes fumbling down the street

EGUNGUN.
>Calling you out your name.

SHANGO.
>It's that bass drop …

O LI ROON.
>So hard, thumping.

EGUNGUN.
>*Dum da da, dum da da!*

OGUN.
>It calls late, as soon as the sun downs

EGUNGUN.
>And again out of nowhere …

ALL.
>A crowd …

EGUNGUN.
>The Egungun assumes the position.
>DJing and spinning tha hottest earth
>Thumping melodies invoking sex and

Heat.
Goddamn look at the girl in the green!
SHUN.
      Shun ...
NIA.
      And Nia ...
SHUN.
      Walk in.
NIA.
      In their best public,
      Yet intimate apparel
SHUN.
      They walk through
SHANGO.
      The men stare!
SHUN.
      How could they not?
EGUNGUN.
      Damn girl in the green came ready to ride
      for real shawty what's real? Oh she acting
      all stank, that's alright you be begging me
      to be your baby daddy later girl.
SHUN.
      You better watch you mouth boy!
EGUNGUN.
      A'ight li'l mama I ain't trying to fight
      Not tonight it's too thick and tight
      Out here. Y'all ready for that next
      One? He plays a song with ride
      In its rhythm, making you wanna grind where
      you are.
      That's it y'all get to that spot.
      Where's it real hot. I'm a keep
      Turning the temperature up
      Y'all just keep riding out
      Specially you li'l red in the green
      you thick as fuck!
OYA.
      Oya hears that beat!

SHUN.

How could she not?

OYA.

She stands and watches.

EGUNGUN.

It's that time of night where
Everyone in the out over here
Needs to get to know that freak within.
You know what I'm talking, 'specially
For the fellas. Come on y'all I got a hundred
Dollars for that freshest freak girl out there.

NIA.

Teasing her friend.
Go 'head girl.

SHUN.

You done lost your mind!

NIA.

That's a hundred dollars.
They say you a freak …

SHUN.

You do it, Nia!

NIA.

Ain't nobody wanna see my stretch marks.

SHUN.

Well I can't in my condition …

EGUNGUN.

A hundred dollars for that nasty girl!
The one who get up here and show us all the world.
C'mon li'l mama do your thang mommy.
Get up here on this speaker box.
We want to see the way you move.
Y'all scared? Why you acting shy?
After this here next song through we gone touch the sky

ELEGBA.

Enter 'Legba beaming like a full moon,
Bright in all white.
He moves to Oya.

OYA.

'Legba …

ELEGBA.
    Oya, what you doing here?
OYA.
    I just came to see …
ELEGBA.
    You sure … just to see?
OYA.
    'Legba where the baby?
ELEGBA.
    My mama got him.
EGUNGUN.
    Appears the Egungun.
    Eh my man 'Legba!
ELEGBA.
    They pull close.
EGUNGUN.
    Too close to be just friends.
ELEGBA and EGUNGUN.
    Just friends.
OYA.
    Oya sees it how could she not.
EGUNGUN.
    The Egungun sees Oya.
    This your friend?
ELEGBA.
    Yeah she is.
EGUNGUN.
    You told her about me, your friend?
    She know we friends?
    She wanna be friends with us?
ELEGBA.
    Smiling like the light of the night.
    Ask her.
EGUNGUN.
    How you doin …
    Oya?
ELEGBA.
    Yeah.
OYA.
    I'm alright.

You pretty …
Everybody tell you that though,
I know they do.
You … you got any kids?
EGUNGUN.
Nah, nah, not yet though.
No.
OYA.
Oya moves to …
EGUNGUN.
Don't go. Let me play this song.
I'll be back … for both of you.
OYA.
'Legba …
ELEGBA.
He will if you wait.
We can go with him …
You been looking, right? You came to see.
Maybe this what you looking for …
Maybe this fix what's broke …
OYA.
Oya walking back.
Turns.
AUNT ELEGUA.
Running into the dancing Aunt Elegua!
UH HUH! THAT'S MY JAM MR. DJ!
Shake that goodness hey! Like taffy laffy!
Work it out! That's what I mean,
Dancing a "too old to be acting this young" dance!
I just cuts it loose y'all, yeah I do, I get it out!
Ooh yeah honey!
OYA.
Laughing how could she not!
AUNT ELEGUA.
What you gone stay here all night Oya!
Girl you betta c'mon and dance it out.
C'mon real hard so you get your system
Cleaned. Work it like this!
OYA.
Oya dances like Elegua.

AUNT ELEGUA.
>Nah gal it's like this here.
>Aunt Elegua gets down with
>Her big old self backing that
>thang up! Uh-huh!
>That's how you do that.

OYA.
>Laughing …
>A cloud passes.
>I don't feel good Aunt Ele'.
>You come to get me?

AUNT ELEGUA.
>Came to show you a way home.

Scene 7

OYA.
>Oya girl sitting on the front porch
>humming and then crying. Smiling.
>Then humming again.

Scene 8

OGUN.
>Ogun Size enters.
>Oya.

OYA.
>You don't need to be there.

OGUN.
>Oya you just hurt.

OYA.
>You don't know …

OGUN.
>Please let's go in …

I'll take care of you.
OYA.
I don't need you to take care of me.
OGUN.
Oya one day we …
OYA.
No! No more days! None!
What you got?
You gone be stuck here like me forever.
Just us so what you got?
What I need you to do for me?
Gone 'head Ogun
Gone 'head …
OGUN.
Ogun turns.
OYA.
You was good to me …
OGUN.
Ogun begins to turn back
OYA.
Don't turn around!
You was good to me,
And I loved you.
Go find somebody who love you better.
Don't … turn.
Gone 'head now …
Gone 'head.
OGUN.
Ogun Size leaves his heart behind.
OYA.
'Legba enters like the moon during the day, there but not
saying anything.
'Legba, 'Legba, 'Legba!
You surprised me!
ELEGBA.
OYA.
I didn't know you was like that!
I didn't know you was into things like that.
I mean I know you got a li'l freak in you …

ELEGBA.

    'Legba smiles.

OYA.

    'Legba.

    You a grey boy?

ELEGBA.

    I got a son.

OYA.

    Grey boys have sons.

ELEGBA.

    I came to tell you …

OYA.

    Don't …

    I don't feel …

ELEGBA.

    Shango is home.

OYA.

    Oya curls …

ELEGBA.

    He coming here I saw him.

    He stopped by Ogun and shook his hand first.

    Say he sorry how he acted before.

    Say now that he grown … He need to say his sorry's.

OYA.

    Huh.

ELEGBA.

    I dream about you Oya.

OYA.

    Gone now 'Legba.

ELEGBA.

    It's always been the same …

OYA.

    Gone!

ELEGBA.

    Elegba walks away, staring at Oya

OYA.

    Shun and Nia enter to give me more bad news.

SHUN.

    Don't …

    No, now!

NIA.

>C'mon on now Shun be a good neighbor!

SHUN.

>>Fuck that ... Fuck that!
>>Under her breath
>>I don't like that ... I don't see why
>>I have to ...
>>She crazy anyway!

NIA.

>>Go on girl stop being like that.
>>To Oya
>>Hey!

OYA.

>>Hey!

SHUN.

>>...

NIA.

>>Shun!

SHUN.

>>Ah shit!
>>I guess you've heard ...

OYA.

>>I know Shango back.

SHUN.

>>Yeah I guess you would know that.
>>But you heard about me?
>>Me and Shango?

OYA.

>>You and Shango what?

SHUN.

>>You better act like you happy for me
>>looking all sad 'n' shit ...
>>You better know.

OYA.

>>Happy for what?

SHUN.

>>Smile

NIA.

>>Shun got Shango's baby.

SHUN.
  I'm having his baby
  So I'm his woman now!
  You ain't shit to him.
NIA.
  Shun!
SHUN.
  Heavy breath!
  But I was gone come to
  Invite you to the shower we having,
  Ifyoucanmakeit. See I said it le's go.
OYA.
  Thank you …
  I don't think I'll be there.
SHUN.
  Good …
  I mean yeah …
  Come on Nia.
OYA.
  Oya's breath comes loose …
SHUN.
  You alright?
OYA.
  Yeah I just gotta go inside
  I gotta get a gift for Shango.
SHUN.
  Where my gift?
OYA.
  You already got it.
NIA.
  Come on Shun.
OYA.
  Oya with light in her eyes
  Enters her house.
NIA.

SHUN.

OYA.
  Nia and Shun leave.

Shango enters
SHANGO.
    He stands in his officer's uniform.
OYA.
(Offstage.)
    You out there now Shango!
    I know you are …
    I be there in a minute!
SHANGO.
    Good to see you Oya gal.
    Take your time …
OYA.
    I know you a busy man now
    I heard your good news,
    I heard your good news!
    So I said let me get him something,
    A present so he remembers me in his new life and times!
SHANGO.
    You didn't have to do that.
OYA.
    Yes I did …
    I have to do it.
ELEGBA.
    'Legba enters like the moon eclipsing the sun
    She sleep now
    But her eyes still open
    Yes sleep now
    But her tears still flowin'
OYA.
    Oya enters
    Holding her hand to her head.
SHANGO.
    Shango moves to curl his fingers.
OYA.
    But Oya's hand …
SHANGO.
    Holding her head …
OYA.
    Is blocking him.

ELEGBA.

    Come down peace
    Come down night
    Cover over Oya girl
    Make her world alright

OYA.

    In the other hand, her left ...
    Oya gives it to Shango.
    I do this in remembrance of you ...
    I wished I could make a part of me
    to give you but I had to take what's
    already there ... Just give you what I got.
    Oya bleeds, down her right hand.

ELEGBA.

    She bleeds now,

SHANGO.

    You ...

OYA.

    Open it ...

ELEGBA.

    Her wounds all close

SHANGO.

    Shango opens his hand ...

ELEGBA.

    She breathes still

OYA.

    Oya moves her hand from where her ear used to be ...

ELEGBA.

    But her belly never rose

OYA.

    For you to remember me by ...

(Oya collapses down.)

ELEGBA.

    Come down peace now
    Come down night
    Cover over Oya girl
    Make her world alright

Epilogue

All save Oya stand, the men hum that sweet sad hum.

Oya, center stage, holding her head.

AUNT ELEGUA.
    I don't know about all that …
SHUN.
    Me neither
MAMA MOJA/NIA/ THE WOMAN THAT.
    No one does …
OYA.
    Oya …
MAMA MOJA/NIA/ THE WOMAN THAT.
    Say she cut it off …
AUNT ELEGUA.
    Say that's her mark.
SHUN.
    Say he left her there bleeding.
OYA.
    A breeze over Oya.
SHUN.
    Somebody called her crazy so and so …
AUNT ELEGUA.
    She wasn't crazy
MAMA MOJA/NIA/ THE WOMAN THAT.
    Just sad.
ALL.
    Huh.
OYA.
    Oya … Oya.
AUNT ELEGUA.
    Say she sitting up somewhere …
OYA.
    Oya …

MAMA MOJA/NIA/ THE WOMAN THAT.
    Staring at the ceiling
OYA.
    Oya girl …
SHUN.
    On her back like a lake of brown …
AUNT ELEGUA/MAMA MOJA/SHUN.
    Staring …
ALL.
    Huh.
MAMA MOJA/NIA/THE WOMAN THAT.
    My lord.
OYA.
    In the air … Oya.
AUNT ELEGUA.
    Holding her head staring at the sky
    You look at her,
    Aunt Elegua looks to Oya,
    Look like she floating somewhere
OYA.
    In the air …
SHUN.
    Oya Jean Fair …
AUNT ELEGUA.
    My girl Oya.
MAMA MOJA/NIA/THE WOMAN THAT.
    Sweet sad Oya.
AUNT ELEGUA/MAMA MOJA/SHUN.
    Beautiful girl.
(Oya lets out a sharp breath.)
OYA.
    Ah!
(Blackout.)

End of Play

PROPERTY LIST

Baby
Clothes, clothesline, clothespins
Bag of groceries

SOUND EFFECTS

Music
Party music